HOW TO DRAW
SCIENCE FICTION

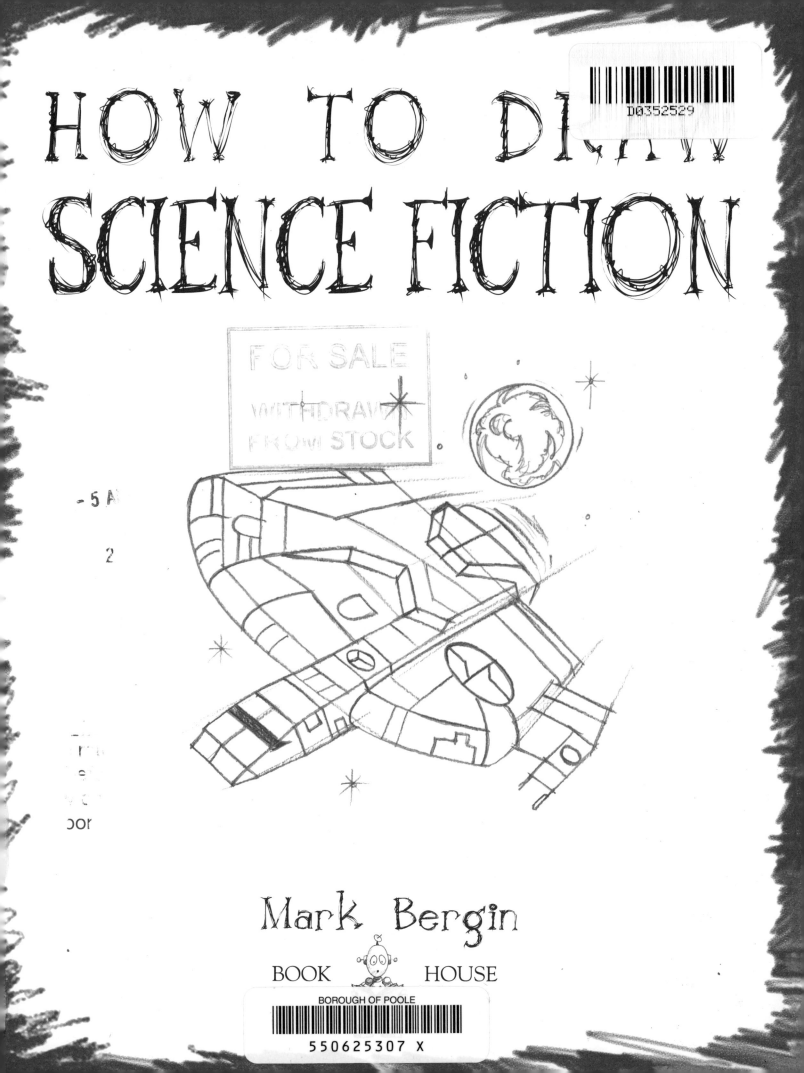

FOR SALE
WITHDRAWN
FROM STOCK

-5 A

2

Mark Bergin

BOOK HOUSE

D0352529

BOROUGH OF POOLE

550625307 X

SALARIYA

© The Salariya Book Company Ltd MMXII
All rights reserved. No part of this book may be
reproduced, stored in a retrieval system or transmitted in
any form or by any means, electronic, mechanical,
photocopying, recording or otherwise, without the written
permission of the copyright owner.

Published in Great Britain in MMXII by
Book House, an imprint of
The Salariya Book Company Ltd
25 Marlborough Place, Brighton BN1 1UB

1 3 5 7 9 8 6 4 2

Please visit our website at **www.book-house.co.uk**
or go to **www.salariya.com** for **free** electronic
versions of:
You Wouldn't Want to be an Egyptian Mummy!
You Wouldn't Want to be a Roman Gladiator!
You Wouldn't Want to be a Polar Explorer!
You Wouldn't Want to sail on a 19th-Century
   Whaling Ship!

Author: Mark Bergin was born in Hastings in 1961.
He studied at Eastbourne College of Art and has
specialised in historical reconstructions as well as
aviation and maritime subjects since 1983. He lives
in Bexhill-on-Sea with his wife and three children.

Editor: Victoria England

PB ISBN: 978-1-907184-64-2

A CIP catalogue record for this
book is available from the
British Library.

Printed and bound in China.
Printed on paper from
sustainable sources.
**WARNING: Fixatives should be
used only under adult supervision.**

Visit our websites to read interactive
free web books, stay up to date with
new releases, catch up with us on
the Book House Blog, view our
electronic catalogue and more!

www.book-house.co.uk
Information books
and graphic novels

www.scribobooks.com
Fiction books

www.scribblersbooks.com
Books for babies, toddlers and
pre-school children.

Follow us on Facebook and
Twitter by visiting
www.salariya.com

PAPER FROM
SUSTAINABLE
FORESTS

Contents

Making a start

Learning to draw is about looking and seeing. Keep practising and get to know your subject. Use a sketchbook to make quick drawings. Start by doodling, and experiment with shapes and patterns. There are many ways to draw; this book shows only some methods. Visit art galleries, look at artists' drawings, see how friends draw, but above all, find your own way.

Remember that practice makes perfect. If it looks wrong, start again. Keep working at it — the more you draw, the more you will learn.

Materials

Try using different types of drawing paper and materials. Experiment with charcoal, wax crayons and pastels. All pens, from felt-tips to ballpoints, will make interesting marks — you could also try drawing with pen and ink on wet paper.

Silhouette is a style of drawing which mainly uses solid black shapes.

Ink silhouette

Lines drawn in **ink** cannot be erased, so keep your ink drawings sketchy and less rigid. Don't worry about mistakes as these lines can be lost in the drawing as it develops.

Ink

Adding light and shade to a drawing with an ink pen can be tricky. Use solid ink for the very darkest areas and cross-hatching (straight lines criss-crossing each other) for ordinary dark tones. Use hatching (straight lines running parallel to each other) for midtones and keep the lightest areas empty.

Hard pencils are greyer and soft pencils are blacker. Hard pencils are graded from 6H (the hardest) through 5H, 4H, 3H and 2H to H.

Soft pencils are graded from B, 2B, 3B, 4B and 5B up to 6B (the softest).

Wax crayons can be scraped away from parts of a drawing to create special effects.

Charcoal is very soft and can be used for big, bold drawings.

Pencil

Felt—tip

Pastels are softer than charcoal and come in a wide range of colours. Ask an adult to spray your pastel drawing with fixative to prevent it from smudging.

Felt—tips come in a range of line widths. The wider pens are good for filling in large areas of flat tone.

7

Perspective

If you look at any object from different viewpoints, you will see that the part that is closest to you looks larger, and the part furthest away from you looks smaller. Drawing in perspective is a way of creating a feeling of depth — of showing three dimensions on a flat surface.

High eye level
(view from above)

V.P.

V.P. = vanishing point

Low eye level
(view from below)

V.P.

V.P.

8

Two-point perspective uses two vanishing points: one for lines running along the length of the object, and one on the opposite side for lines running across the width of the object.

Three-point perspective drawings use three vanishing points. This method is good for drawing a figure from a more dramatic angle.

It may help you with perspective if you imagine that your figure fits into a rectangular block like this.

The vanishing point (V.P.) is the place in a perspective drawing where parallel lines appear to meet. The position of the vanishing point depends on the viewer's eye level. Sometimes a low viewpoint can give your drawing added drama.

9

Places and planets

Be imaginative when drawing places in space. Try to make the landscapes and settings as exciting or unusual as possible.

Roughly sketch construction lines for your drawings to help you.

Experiment by changing the eye level and vanishing points of your drawings (see page 8) to create a sense of drama.

Once you have the basic shape of the drawing you can start to add windows and other final details.

Use hatching to create
the texture of rock.

Draw stars and planets in the sky.

Try to draw something
interesting in both the
foreground and background.

To make your drawing look three-dimensional,
decide which side the light is coming from
so you can put in areas of shadow.

Spacecraft

Space travellers use all sorts of unusual flying machines to move around space. Just like cars and planes today, they come in many different shapes and sizes.

Add a space traveller inside the cockpit of the spacecraft.

Start by drawing the basic shapes.

Use bold, sweeping curves to the shapes to make it look futuristic.

Draw two oval shapes joined together by a smaller rectangle.

Shade areas to make it appear three-dimensional.

Use perspective (see pages 8—9) to make the craft look as though it is hurtling through space.

Round off the corners of the shapes.

Use a mixture of rounded and geometric shapes.

Soft pencil lines coming from the engines give the impression of travelling at speed.

Shade the bottom of the tube shapes to make them appear three-dimensional.

Add two windows for two separate pilots.

Sketch in three rectangular shapes coming out of a larger circle to create an unusual craft shape.

Add detail to the feet.

Be imaginative with the basic shapes to start off with.

Add shading to areas that light would not reach.

For detail, use dark shading to indicate any areas in the bodywork that go inward.

13

Vehicles

People in space drive various types of vehicles to jet between planets and travel around the galaxy. Some are designed for speed, some for comfort and some even for combat.

For this space scooter, start by sketching a large oval shape with a triangle at the front.

Add curved lines and rounded shapes for the detail of the vehicle.

Draw an oval for the head, with helmet detail.

Add tube shapes for limbs.

Draw circles for the joints.

Sketch triangle shapes on the front of the machine.

Shade the front of the vehicle to look like glass.

Complete the detail of the driver by shading in the helmet and making his suit look futuristic.

Shade in the areas where light would not reach.

Remove any unwanted construction lines.

For the space car, start by sketching a large oval shape with a curved line through it where the side of the car meets the top.

Add a spoiler to the rear of the vehicle.

Draw basic rounded shapes on the front.

Make the shape at the front three-dimensional.

Sketch in the outline of the window.

Add curved lines.

Inside the cockpit, add the outline of two chairs and, using basic shapes, a pilot.

Shade the underside of the spoiler.

Shade in the driver and add hair and glasses.

Use soft shading to add detail to the inside of the cockpit.

Add shade to the underside of the vehicle.

Complete the vehicle by shading in the areas where light would not reach.

Space stations

Space stations allow humans to live in outer space for a period of time, mainly carrying out scientific research and experiments. Be as creative as you like with your design.

Start by drawing basic shapes. Make some parts rounded and some geometric.

Add shading to the shapes to make them look three-dimensional.

Notice how the design is built up from larger and smaller versions of the same basic shape.

Be imaginative with the shape of the space station.

This one is built on an asteroid.

Shade the lower part to create the effect of rock.

Finish off by adding detail to the outside of the station.

Draw the shape at an angle to make it look as though it is floating in space.

Remember to remove any unwanted construction lines.

Human characters

Drawing a human science-fiction character can be broken down into easy stages. Follow the steps shown here to create your own astronauts and space explorers.

Start by sketching these simple shapes.

Draw circle and oval shapes for the head, main body and hips.

Add hair.

Use straight guidelines and a vertical centre line to experiment with the proportions of the body.

Draw straight lines for the limbs and circles for the joints.

Then, start to build up the basic shapes and features of the figure.

Change the stance of the figure by moving the straight lines of the limbs.

Turn the lines of the arms and legs into simple tube shapes.

Use construction lines to position the features of the face.

Don't be afraid to exaggerate the features for comic effect.

Helmets must be worn when travelling in space.

Leave a vertical stripe of white when shading the visors. This is the light reflecting off the tinted glass.

Think about how the helmet would look in profile.

Add detail to the surface of the clothing to make it look as futuristic as possible.

Complete the detail of the faces.

Experiment with different facial expressions and body poses.

Sketch a circle and inner rings on the shoulders.

Draw a belt with pouches for tools.

Add a stripe detail to the helmets.

Shade in a suggestion of rocky ground.

Shade the areas where light would not reach.

Draw futuristic boots with large turn-ups.

19

Robots and droids

Robots are artificial, electronic machines which are often found in science—fiction books and films. Androids are designed to look and act like humans and can be very intelligent.

This detail looks a little like a circuit board. Add some to your drawing to make it look more robotic.

Try to make faces from unusual shapes. Use buttons, dials and switches.

Small circles can look like bolts that are holding the robot together.

Add dots and lines to the robot's metalwork to add interest.

Shade some areas where the light would not reach.

Robots' hands can have fingers or be more mechanical.

Start by drawing three large circles and two smaller ones for the robot's body.

Be imaginative with the basic shapes. You could take inspiration from animals, like this insect-like robot.

Add a rectangular breastplate.

These two tube shapes are overlapping to show how one leg passes in front of the other.

Add circles in the joint positions.

Add tube shapes for the legs.

Add detail to the body.

Sketch in basic hand shapes.

Draw in pointed shapes for the feet.

Add fingers.

Shade in areas where the light would not reach.

Add circles to the joints to make them look more mechanical.

21

Space machinery

Space machines are used for exploring new planets. Their powerful legs can keep them steady when travelling over difficult and dangerous terrain. The driver controls the machine from the inside.

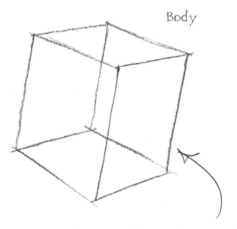

Body

Draw a three-dimensional box for the main body of the space machine.

Sketch in the legs using straight lines to create three-dimensional boxes.

Use a ruler if you like to make lines straight.

Using a mirror
Hold your picture up to a mirror so you can look at it in reverse. This will help you to see mistakes.

Draw two rectangles to form the base of the feet.

Add rectangle shapes to the shoulders.

Using straight lines and circles, sketch in the shape of the arms.

Draw basic rectangular shapes for the window on the front of the machine.

Add the knee joints by drawing two circles and some straight lines.

Add a driver inside the cockpit of the space machine.

Complete the elbow, making the joint look mechanical.

Add fingers.

Decide where the light is coming from, then shade the areas where it would not reach.

Add detail to the machine. Straight lines on its surface show how it is mechanically made.

Add shading to create craters and a rocky terrain.

Alien characters

In science fiction, aliens are creatures that do not come from planet Earth. No—one knows what they really look like, so use your imagination to create your own crazy space alien.

Draw two ovals slightly overlapping.

Add snake—like shapes for tentacles.

Draw in two parallel lines for the base of the top oval.

Draw in some eyes on stalks and shade the oval to look like glass.

Sketch in branch—like shapes for the arms.

Add detail to the body.

Shade the areas where light would not reach.

Add a scaly pattern to the tentacles.

Draw unusually shaped heads to create bizarre alien forms.

Some aliens have more than two eyes.

Add ferocious, sharp teeth.

You could take inspiration from the feaures of dinosaurs.

Add darker parts of shading to the drawing for dramatic effect.

Add wing shapes.

Science—fiction aliens come in all different shapes and sizes.

Stretch out arms and legs to make spidery alien body shapes.

25

Cartoon aliens

There are no rules when drawing aliens. Add extra eyes and legs, draw hands with three fingers or draw the neck very long and skinny. Perhaps even add a flying saucer!

To make this one-eyed alien, start by drawing two ovals joined by a long tube shape.

Add two rounded shapes for feet.

Draw curved lines for arm shapes.

Add shading to the areas where light would not reach.

Draw in markings on the alien's body.

Add one large eye and shading.

Add details to the feet.

Sketch in the toes.

Here is a cute alien with his own flying saucer.

To start with draw two basic ovals and a semi-circle.

Mark in the mouth.

Add five small ovals for the alien's eyes.

Draw more oval shapes at the arms and neck.

Draw in small rounded shapes on the bottom of the flying saucer.

Sketch in two alien antennae.

Mark in the eyes.

Add ear shapes to the side of the head.

Draw in the detail on the face.

Draw curved shapes for two arms.

Shade in the areas where light would not reach.

Draw in the fuel tank on the front of the saucer.

Add the exhaust underneath the flying saucer.

Remove any unwanted construction lines.

27

Spaceman and robots

This spaceman loves to explore new planets, especially when he stumbles across new and interesting alien robots!

Draw two large circles slightly overlapping.

Draw in a visor shape on the helmet.

Sketch in two curved arm shapes.

Shade in the visor, leaving a spot white for a highlight.

Add detail to the face of the spaceman.

Draw in curved leg shapes.

Draw in fingers.

Add basic rounded shapes for the feet.

Indicate the shape of an oxygen pack.

Add shading and detail to the space suit.

Draw vertical lines on the base of the space boots.

Start by drawing basic rounded shapes for the outlines of the two robots.

You can use different-sized shapes to create different characters.

Add circles to mark the positions of the arms.

Add an antenna.

Add rounded shapes with circle knee joints.

Draw eyes and a mouth.

Draw in rounded foot shapes.

Shade the robots to look like shiny metal.

Add branch shapes for arms.

Add the arms using straight lines and circle shapes.

Shade the areas where light would not reach.

29

Cartoon scene

To make your space character drawings even more exciting, you can place the aliens and astronauts in a scene. This can give your drawing added drama and a sense of action. This example shows the characters meeting on an alien planet, but you can use your imagination to draw them in any situation you like.

First draw a box with a horizon line running through it, then draw the construction lines of the characters themselves. Any vanishing points (see pages 8—9) should be on the horizon line.

Draw in simple shapes for
planets in the background.

Sketch in the basic shapes of the spaceman and
aliens and mark the positions of their features.

Once you have the basic shape of the drawing,
you can start to add detail. Add stars in the
sky and craters on the ground.

Draw in the final detail
of the space characters.

31

Glossary

Composition The arrangement of the parts of a picture on the drawing paper.

Construction lines Guidelines used in the early stages of a drawing. They are usually erased later.

Fixative A type of resin used to spray over a finished drawing to prevent smudging. **It should only be used by an adult.**

Light source The direction from which the light seems to come in a drawing.

Perspective A method of drawing in which near objects are shown larger than faraway objects to give an impression of depth.

Pose The position assumed by a figure.

Proportion The correct relationship of scale between each part of the drawing.

Silhouette A drawing that shows only a flat dark shape, like a shadow.

Vanishing point The place in a perspective drawing where parallel lines appear to meet.

Index